Celebrating your year

1963

a very special year for

_____

_____
_____
_____
_____

A message from the author:

Welcome to the year 1963.

I trust you will enjoy this fascinating romp down memory lane.

And when you have reached the end of the book, please join me in the battle against AI generated copy-cat books and fake reviews.

Details are at the back of the book.*

Best regards,
Bernard Bradforsand-Tyler.

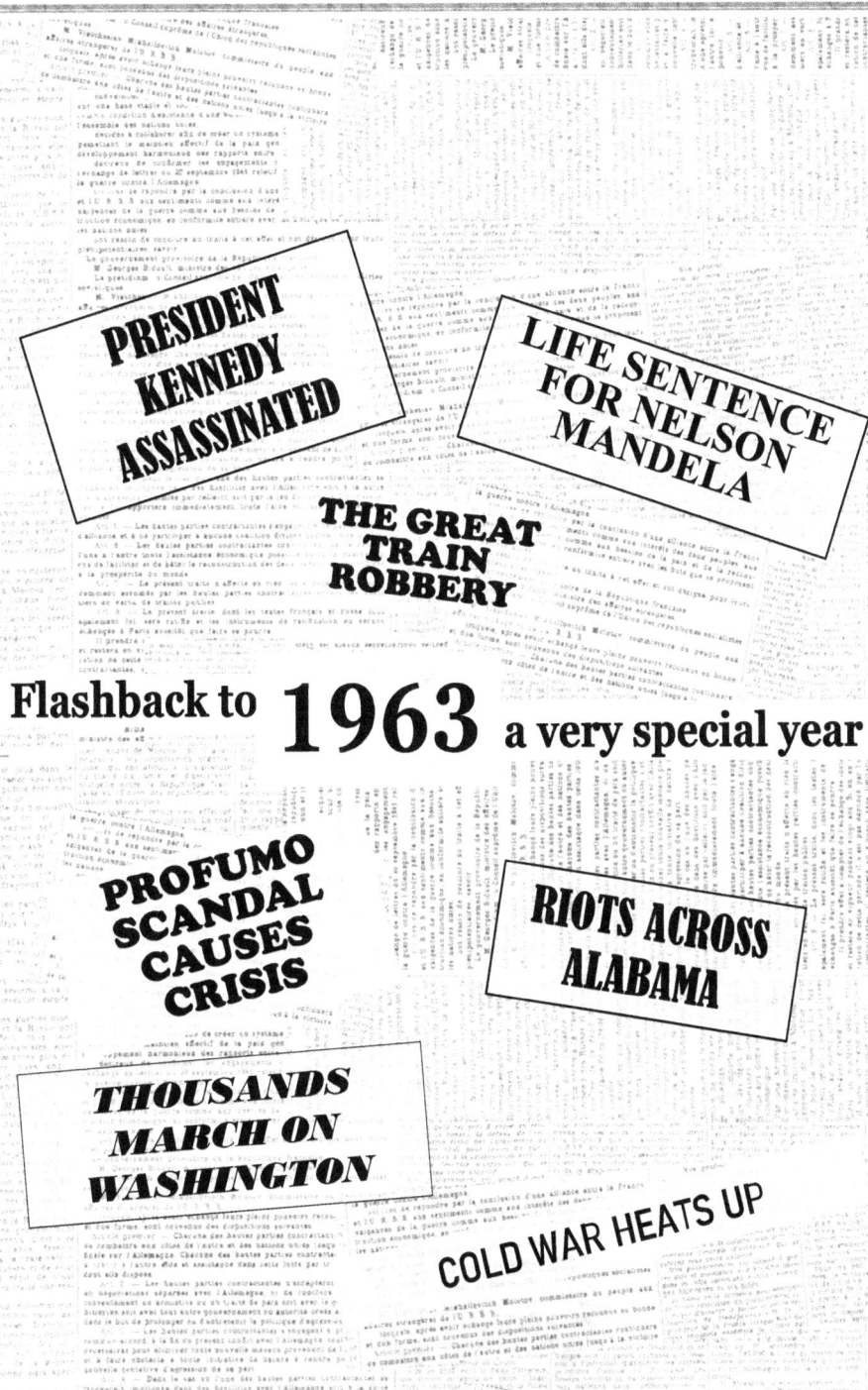

Contents

1963 Family Life in the USA	9
Life in the United Kingdom	14
Our Love Affair with Cars	19
Tuning in to Television	25
Most Popular TV Shows of 1963	26
President Kennedy Assassinated	30
Cold War–Nuclear Arms Race	33
Cold War–Space Race	34
Cold War–Battlefield Vietnam	35
The Summer of Our Discontent	38
March on Washington	40
Life Sentence for Mandela	42
The Profumo Crisis	44
The Great Train Robbery	45
Who Were The Rat Pack?	47
1963 in Cinema and Film	48
Top Grossing Films of the Year	49
A Decade of Cinema Epics	50
Musical Memories	53
1963 Billboard Top 30 Songs	54
Fashion Trends of the 1960s	57
Technology and Medicine	65
Also in Sports	67
Other News from 1963	68
Famous People Born in 1963	72
1963 in Numbers	76
Image Attributions	84

Advertisement

Good grades don't grow on trees.

They grow out of you. A Royal portable just makes it easier. It takes over the mechanics of writing. Frees those 10 billion cells in your brain to think. Thoughts are clearer, work more organized. Compositions become more creative, neater. Words you never used before come to you and fatten up your vocabulary.

With a Royal, misspellings are apparent. Thus, spelling improves. Even your penmanship imitates the very neatness of the printed letter.

In short, a Royal brings out the best in you. But beware. Don't buy a portable that defeats the purpose. Only Royal portables are simplest to use. They are the most helpful.

With the Safari above, for instance, you can set margins and columns as easily as pressing a doorbell, change a ribbon by merely replacing a cartridge.

In sum, Royal portables are easiest to get along with. They're ruggedly built of steel, have a full-sized keyboard and the liveliest keys (hand-fitted) of any portable.

Give Mom the shiny apples to make the pie and let a Royal help you make the grade. See all the Royal models. There are lots of good-looking colors. Maybe you'll like the shiny red one. Royal portables start at $49.95, attractive case included.

Every year more Royal typewriters are bought in America than any other brand.

Let's flashback to 1963, a very special year.

Was this the year you were born?

Was this the year you were married?

Whatever the reason, this book is a celebration of your year,

THE YEAR 1963.

Turn the pages to discover a book packed with fun-filled
fabulous facts. We look at the people, the places, the
politics and the pleasures that made 1963 unique
and helped shape the world we know today.

So get your time-travel suit on, and enjoy this trip down memory
lane, to rediscover what life was like, back in the year 1963.

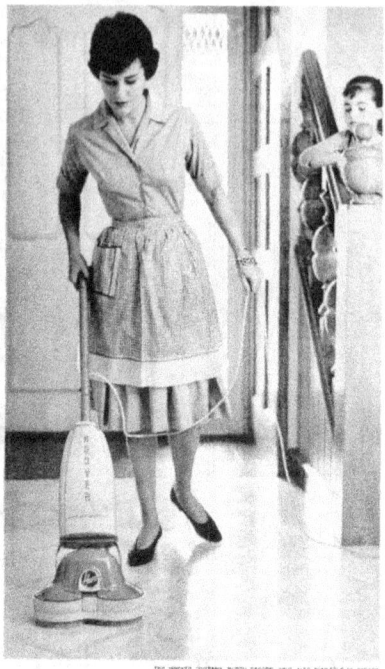

Shampoo a rug today, shine a floor tomorrow —this Hoover does both jobs easy as pie

Now you can have the cleanest rugs, the shiniest floors you've ever had in your life—and all with one appliance. And this Hoover does the heavy work, not you.

Shampooing a rug? Just pull the sudsing trigger and run the Shampoo-Polisher over the rug. Drying's quick because this Hoover does the cleaning job with foam. Water doesn't soak your rug, so it's bright and fresh again in no time.

Polishing or waxing a floor? Another job this Hoover takes in stride. No wax splashing, no corners missed, no heavy work. Built-in wax dispensing tanks make the job even easier.

(Try this work-saving Hoover on your heavy scrubbing, too. You'll find it loosens the stickiest dirt. Takes the strain off your hands and back.)

The price? Low enough to say you can save more than the amount on the price tag the first few times you use this versatile Hoover. Don't you think you should have one?

HOOVER.
QUALITY FLOOR CARE FOR PEOPLE WHO CARE

Shampoo a rug today, shine a floor tomorrow—this Hoover does both jobs easy as pie

Now you can have the cleanest rugs, the shiniest floors you've ever had in your life—and all with one appliance. And this Hoover does the heavy work, not you.

Shampooing a rug? Just pull the sudsing trigger and run the Shampoo-Polisher over the rug. Drying's quick because this Hoover does the cleaning job with foam. Water doesn't soak your rug, so it's bright and fresh again in no time.

Polishing or waxing a floor? Another job this Hoover takes in stride. No wax splashing, no corners missed, no heavy work. Built-in wax dispensing tanks make the job even easier.

(Try this work-saving Hoover on your heavy scrubbing, too. You'll find it loosens the stickiest dirt. Takes the strain off your hands and back.)

The price? Low enough to say you can save more than the amount on the price tag the first few times you use this versatile Hoover. Don't you think you should have one?

Hoover   Quality Floor Care for People Who Care

Family Life in 1963 America

Imagine if time-travel was a reality, and one fine morning you wake up to find yourself flashed back in time, back to the year 1963.

What would life be like for a typical family, in a typical town, somewhere in America?

A stylish modern suburban family kitchen in 1963.

The year 1963 was a turbulent year for Americans. It was a year of political and social tensions. The Civil Rights Movement was in full swing. Protests, riots, and bloodshed spilled into our homes via the news on TV and radio. By year's end, President Kennedy would be assassinated, and his killer shot dead within days.

Yet we often reminisce about this period as a time of prosperity, when babies were born in record numbers, fathers had jobs for life, and our standard of living surpassed that which our parents only dreamed of. A culture of consume and discard flourished, driven by an advertising industry which instilled in us the belief that we constantly needed more and more, bigger and better.

The start of the decade marked a high point for the Baby Boomer generation (1946-1964). Children under nineteen represented 39% of our nation,[1] a percentage which has been in decline ever since.

The single income family was still the norm, with fathers commuting to work while mothers were encouraged to stay at home.

Children riding bicycles in a suburban street.

One-third of us lived in the suburbs, having fled the decaying cities for the dream of a house on our own land, a car, a dog and 2.3 kids. 80% of households owned an automobile. The 40-hour workweek with paid leave had become the norm and we spent more on leisure activities, health care and education than ever before.

[1] www2.census.gov/library/publications/1963/demographics/P25-276.pdf.

For women, marriage and children were still the priority. Most women aged 30-34 were married (87%) and the majority (90%) had children.[1]

Working women could expect to be paid almost 40% less than their male counterparts. It was universally accepted that a man was the breadwinner of the family, and that a wife should earn less.

Mother with children in the kitchen, 1963.

The median family income was $6,200 a year.[2] Unemployment stood at 5.5%, with GDP growth at 4.4%.[3]

Average costs in 1963 [4]	
New house	$19,785
New car	$3,235
Washing machine	$170
Vacuum cleaner	$35
A gallon of gasoline	$0.31

[1] From the US Census Bureau-1960 Census: Population, Supplementary Reports: Marital Status of the Population.
[2] census.gov/library/publications/1963/demo/p60-040.html.
[3] thebalance.com/unemployment-rate-by-year-3305506.
[4] thepeoplehistory.com and mclib.info/reference/local-history-genealogy/historic-prices/.

But beyond the glamour and excesses of our pristine, appliance-filled suburban lives, there was another America. One where struggles with poverty, health care, education, housing, racial and sexual inequality, and even the right to vote were brewing the demand for change.

African Americans, women, and other minorities were amplifying their voices. We took to the streets in record numbers—demanding to be heard, demanding change for a better, more egalitarian America. The 1960s would become the decade of reform and revolution.

Protestors march to the Lincoln Memorial, Washington DC. 28th Aug 1963.

Adding to the unrest, Cold War politics dominated our lives. The war in Vietnam was increasing its pull on US soldiers, weapons and funding, while the Nuclear Arms Race and the Space Race were in full swing. We stockpiled nuclear weapons at a frenzied pace, testing bombs at sea, in the air, and underground. Meanwhile, space exploration was turning outer-space into the next Cold War battleground. We would endure another three decades of tensions between the two superpowers before the Cold War finally ended with the dissolution of the Soviet Union in 1991.

Advertisement

Taste the delicious difference —only in new Montclair!

Only Montclair puts the menthol in the filter...where it cannot burn.
Only Montclair filters in freshness, filters in flavor the whole smoke through.
Only Montclair makes the last puff taste as fresh as the first puff.
Taste and compare—you'll smoke **Montclair! Only Montclair.**

Taste the delicious difference—only in new Montclair!
Only Montclair puts the menthol in the filter... where it cannot burn.
Only Montclair filters in freshness, filters in flavor the whole smoke through.
Only Montclair makes the last puff taste as fresh as the first puff.
Taste and compare—you'll smoke Montclair! Only Montclair.
The menthol's in the filter—not in the tobacco!
Important: Montclair gives you a unique development in Compound Filters created by The American Tobacco Company.
Product of The American Tobacco Company... "Tobacco is our middle name."

Life in the United Kingdom

Now just imagine you flashed back to a town in 1963 England or Western Europe.

Unlike their lavish, consumer-driven counterparts in America, a very different picture would await you.

By 1963, the United Kingdom was still struggling to regain its place on the world stage. It was no longer a superpower, having lost that title, along with many of its former colonies, in the aftermath of the second world war. Rebuilding from the ruins of war had exacted a heavy economic toll on the country.

The year began with one of the coldest winters on record. Known as "The Big Freeze", blizzards and plummeting temperatures saw much of England, Wales and Scotland covered in snow for ten full weeks. Rivers, lakes and even the coastal sea froze over. Up to 700 people died during the winter from respiratory tract infections caused by the severe toxic smog of December '62, and exacerbated by the winter's influenza epidemic.

London "Bobby" helping kids cross the street.

Yet beneath the bleakness, austerity and stoicism, the country was bursting with a resurgence of youthful vitality and dynamism unlike anything it had known before. Artists, writers, academics and musicians were developing their own uniquely British creations, and were ready to explode onto the global stage.

By year's end, British youth would lead the cultural revolution of the '60s, and London would be their epicenter. A more expressive, tolerant and open-minded view of society had been born. It would filter through the streets of London, and the cultural revolution known as the "Swinging Sixties" would, through music, fashion and the arts, place Britain once again at the center of the world.

Musicians led the charge with their own uniquely British sound. Influenced by American rock 'n' roll of the '50s, yet infused with innovative new sounds, their songs inspired their fans to break free from conservative norms, to express their individuality.

The Beatles with Ed Sullivan. From left: Ringo Starr, George Harrison, Sullivan, John Lennon, and Paul McCartney, 9th Feb 1964.

Mary Quant with husband Alexander Plunket Greene, 1963.

In fashion, designer Mary Quant created youthful styles for running, jumping and dancing in. Along with other trend-setting designers, the fashion scene centered around London's Carnaby Street and King's Road in Kensington.

In literature, retired British spy Jean Le Carré penned unstoppable mystery thrillers infused with cold-war espionage. His books, along with crowd-pleasing favorites from British authors Agatha Christie, Alistair MacLean, Victor Canning and others, became instant International best sellers.

Advertisement

Presented by a neighbor in the interest of your children's future

Have you looked into your children's future lately? Have you looked over their shoulders recently? Then you are keenly aware of their urgent need for preparation, for encouragement, for help. You can give all three... when you give World Book Encyclopedia.

World Book is far more than a fact-filled 20-volume reference set. Page by page, article by article, it has been carefully created to supplement school work, help bring out the best in any student, increase his chances for success. No wonder World Book is chosen for more homes, schools, and libraries than any other encyclopedia!

To add interest and understanding, World Book sparkles with more than 22,400 illustrations—almost 6,000 in color—and 1,725 maps. More than 2,500 authorities contribute to its excellence and accuracy. For extra value, World Book gives you five more volumes than other sets at comparable prices.

Have a chat with your neighborhood World Book Encyclopedia representative, trained to help you to help your children. Neither minutes nor money could ever be better invested.

World Book Encyclopedia 20 volumes—Aristocrat Binding $182.30
Cyclo-teacher Learning Aid. An easy to use teaching machine with more than 40 Study Cycles in Science, Arithmetic, Geography, Spelling, Grammar, and Sports and Hobbies.

By 1963, private car ownership was still rare, and most households continued to rely on public transport. In fact, steam trains continued to run until the mid-'60s. Road networks and telecommunications remained woefully inadequate.

Early '60s photo of lady on a double-decker bus.

Piccadilly Circus in the early '60s.

90% of British power was supplied by coal, with inner city power stations, factories and domestic fireplaces belching out sulfur-laden smoke.

In the years leading up to 1963 the UK, like much of the western world, enjoyed low unemployment (around 2%), real wage increases, and consumer spending growth. There was spare money for luxuries and leisure pursuits. Prime Minister Harold MacMillan famously summed it up when he stated, "you've never had it so good".[1]

The UK's apparent prosperity masked the relative decline of British competitiveness on the world stage. The UK had slipped far behind its European neighbors and did not come close to the lavish consumerism of the USA. Post war Britain had borrowed heavily from USA and Canada in order to survive and rebuild. Yet Britain failed to modernize its industries in the same way France, Germany, and other war-torn countries had succeeded in doing. In the year 2006, Britain finally paid back the last of its post war loans.

[1] nationalarchives.gov.uk/education/resources/fifties-britain/youve-never-good/.

Advertisement

Your pulse rate goes up whenever you see one of these? Relax–you're perfectly normal.

There's nothing we enjoy more than watching someone take a close look at one of our GPs for the first time. The small, admiring shake of the head. The pursed lips of judicious approval. The sudden turn to a companion to share one's appreciation. All these we see, time and again. We flush a little with pleased pride. We made that! we want to shout. It's a Grand Prix and it comes with a 306-bhp Trophy V-8 and easy-chair bucket seats and a console and just take another look at those utterly clean lines, we babble silently. A lot of people must hear us, though. There are GPs all over the place

Pontiac Grand Prix

Our Love Affair with Cars

By 1963, 68.7 million cars were on our roads. And with more and more cars purchased each year, owning a car was no longer considered a luxury reserved only for the wealthy.

Chevy dealer's lot in 1963.

Increased car ownership and the creation of the National Highway System gave us a new sense of freedom. Office commuters could live further out from city centers and commute quickly and comfortably to work. The suburbanization of America, which began in the early '50s, now saw one-third of Americans living in the suburbs. Furthermore, rural areas were no longer isolated, benefiting from access to food, medical and other supplies.

Services related businesses such as drive-through or drive-in restaurants and drive-in cinemas were commonplace and popular, especially among the younger generation.

[1] fhwa.dot.gov/ohim/summary95/mv200.pdf.

Advertisement

The economical Newport 4-door sedan

$2,964.*

and we can prove it.

A full-size Chrysler for only $2964? A 5-year or 50,000-mile warranty?** A husky V-8 engine that actually prefers regular gas? Lush fabrics? Carpeting? All this for $2964? To some people, the crisp, custom, luxury look of Chrysler suggests a price far above that surprisingly low $2964.

If you happen to be such a person, we'd like you to size up Chrysler your own way. Take your own good time. Compare facts, figures and features with any car in any showroom in town. We think you'll agree that a $2964 Chrysler is the best value in view ... anywhere.

Can't believe it? Then walk up to your nearest Chrysler dealer and make him prove it!

*Manufacturer's suggested retail price of Newport 4-door sedan, exclusive of state and local taxes, if any, and destination charges. White wall tires extra. **Your authorized Chrysler Dealer's 5 warranty against defects in material and workmanship on 1963 cars has been expanded to include parts replacement or repair, without charge for required parts or labor, for 5 years or 50,000 miles, whichever comes first, on the engine block, head and internal parts; transmission case and internal parts (excluding manual clutch); torque converter, drive shaft, universal joints (excluding dust covers), rear axle and differential, and rear wheel bearings, provided the vehicle has been serviced at reasonable intervals according to the Chrysler Certified Car Care schedule.

CHRYSLER

$2,964. and we can prove it.

A full-size Chrysler for only $2964? A 5-year or 50,000-mile warranty? A husky V-8 engine that actually prefers regular gas? Lush fabrics? Carpeting? All this for $2964? To some people, the crisp, custom, luxury look of Chrysler suggests a price far above that surprisingly low $2964.

  If you happen to be such a person, we'd like you to size up Chrysler your own way. Take your own good time. Compare facts, figures and features with any car in any showroom in town. We think you'll agree that a $2964 Chrysler is the best value in view... anywhere.

  Can't believe it? Then walk up to your nearest Chrysler dealer and make him prove it!

An astonishing one in six working adults were employed directly or indirectly by the American automobile industry.

1963 Mercury Monterey S-55 2-door hardtop.

Detroit was America's car manufacturing powerhouse, where "the Big Three" (Ford, General Motors and Chrysler) produced year-on-year bigger, longer, and heavier gas-guzzlers to satisfy the midcentury consumer desire for style over efficiency and safety. Decorative chrome and tail fins reached new heights towards the end of the '50s. However, by the early '60s, the consumer mentality began turning against this extravagance and excess.

Led in part by the success of the imported Volkswagen Beetle and the economic recession of 1958, consumer demand began shifting towards smaller, more compact, cheaper and safer vehicles.

The scene was set for Japanese small car manufacturers to take on the Big Three.

Above: 1963 Super Torque Ford Convertible.
Below: 1963 Dodge Dart by Chrysler.

Four car-producing countries dominated in 1963: England, France, and Germany, with America in the top spot. However, this elite group would soon be rocked by the aggressive expansion of the Japanese automotive industry. Within a few years, Japan would rise to become the second largest car producing country, behind only the US.

1963 European car advertisements:
Top left: Fiat 1100. Top right: Volkswagen Beetle. Above: Renault R8.

Car ownership in other countries lagged behind the USA, even with the rising incomes and living standards of most western nations. Public transport was still the norm for European and British commuters.

In Asia, the car had yet to become mainstream. Less than 1% of the population in China and India could afford a car.

Advertisement

Cadillac Ladies Love to Play Chauffeur.

Unusual? Not at all.

For this one is really fun to drive... feather-light and sure to handle... smooth and effortless on the move... quick and nimble in the clutches. The reasons are mostly man-talk: a high performance engine, a true center drive line, a triple braking system, graduated power steering. But the result is eloquent enough for any lady to understand: the finest, sweetest performance in any automobile today. Visit your dealer soon and see for yourself. And bring your loveliest chauffeur with you.

Advertisement

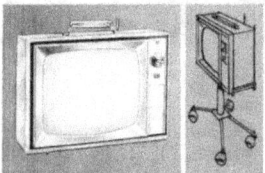 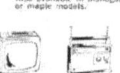  

Now... a TV that needs less "doctoring"
New Truetone *instant* television!
Switch on, show's on... with Insta-Vu

Picture and sound come alive instantly when you flip the switch on this new Truetone "Insta-Vu" 23" Imperial console. No annoying wait for warm-ups... no fidgeting to see what show is coming on! Convenient? Yes. But that's not all.

Insta-Vu helps protect delicate tube filaments by reducing warm-up power surge. Keeps out damaging moisture for smoother chassis operation. Truetone "instant" TV lets you see *more* TV... *less* of the repairman.

New 20,000-volt Kimcode picture tube minimizes annoying reflections. Shatterproof, too! Power transformer and 3-stage I.F. chassis assure strong, clear reception even in fringe areas. Features twin speakers, plus realism of FM sound! Buy now on easy terms, no money down... at W.A.!

Offering outstanding values with satisfaction guaranteed or your money back...
Western Auto

Tuning in to Television

Television ownership in America soared during the '50s and early '60s, increasing sharply from only 9% of households in 1950, to 91% by 1963. During the '50s, television's "Golden Age", most of the programs were broadcast live from New York in the ongoing tradition of old-time radio broadcasting. But by the '60s, made-for-TV programs coming out of Los Angeles dominated our screens.

By 1963, the three national US television networks were able to reach the most remote parts of the country, bringing a shared common experience to both urban and rural America. Television had quickly become our preferred source of entertainment and information.

TV time in the early '60s.

Elsewhere in the world, access to television was not nearly as widespread as in the US. Due to the extreme costs of setting up networks and financing programs, many countries did not begin television broadcasts until the mid-'60s or later.

Most Popular TV Shows of 1963

1	The Beverly Hillbillies	11	The Red Skelton Show
2	Bonanza	12	I've Got a Secret
3	The Dick Van Dyke Show	=	Lassie
4	Petticoat Junction	=	The Jack Benny Show
5	The Andy Griffith Show	15	The Jackie Gleason Show
6	The Lucy Show	16	The Donna Reed Show
7	Candid Camera	17	The Virginian
8	The Ed Sullivan Show	18	The Patty Duke Show
9	The Danny Thomas Show	19	Dr. Kildare
10	My Favorite Martian	20	Gunsmoke

* From the Nielsen Media Research 1963-'64 season of top-rated primetime TV series in the USA.

By 1963, the dominance of dramatic Westerns had given way to the frivolity of variety programs, game shows and sitcoms. Seven of the top 10 programs for the year were situation comedies, following the format of 1950s sitcom sensation *I Love Lucy*.

The Lucy Show was Lucille Ball's follow-up to *I Love Lucy*, securing her two Emmy Awards during its six-year run.

Lucille Ball and Vivian Vance in *The Lucy Show* (CBS. 1962-1968).

Mary Tyler Moore & Dick Van Dyke in *The Dick Van Dyke Show* (CBS. 1961-1966).

CBS sitcom *The Dick Van Dyke Show* ran for five seasons, turning Dick Van Dyke and Mary Tyler Moore into household names.

Both *The Lucy Show* and *The Dick Van Dyke Show* were filmed by Desilu Studios (Lucille Ball and Desi Arnaz) using their 3-camera multiple angle technique. The two shows were the only sitcoms of the time to be filmed in front of live studio audiences.

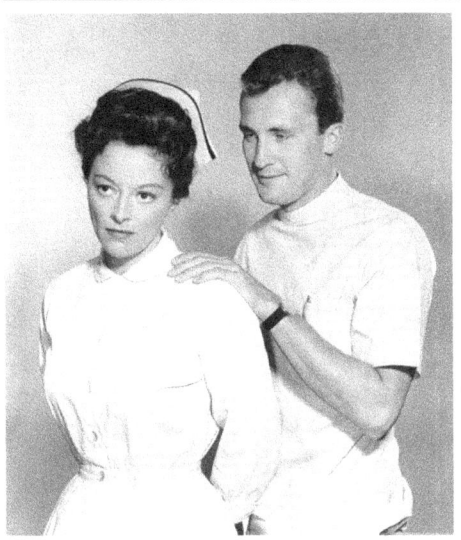
Emily McLaughlin and Roy Thinnes in *General Hospital* (ABC. 1963-present).

Jeannine Riley, Linda Kaye and Pat Woodell in *Petticoat Junction* (CBS. 1963-1970).

The television networks were quick to turn out new programs to keep us tuning in. Here are just a few of the new programs that aired for the first time in 1963: *General Hospital* (1963-present), *Petticoat Junction, My Favorite Martian, Let's Make a Deal, The Dick Emery Show, New Faces,* and *Doctor Who* (UK, BBC).

Ray Walston as Uncle Martin O'Hara in *My Favorite Martian* (CBS. 1963-'65).

William Hartnell as the first Doctor in *Doctor Who* (BBC. 1963-'89 & 2005-present).

ye Indians are hungry tonight!

Be a friendly Pilgrim and serve your little tribe a real turkey dinner. Besides tender slices of succulent turkey, there's old-fashioned dressing, fresh-tasting peas, and mashed potatoes. Expensive? Indeed, no! Just *tastes* expensive!

Advertisement

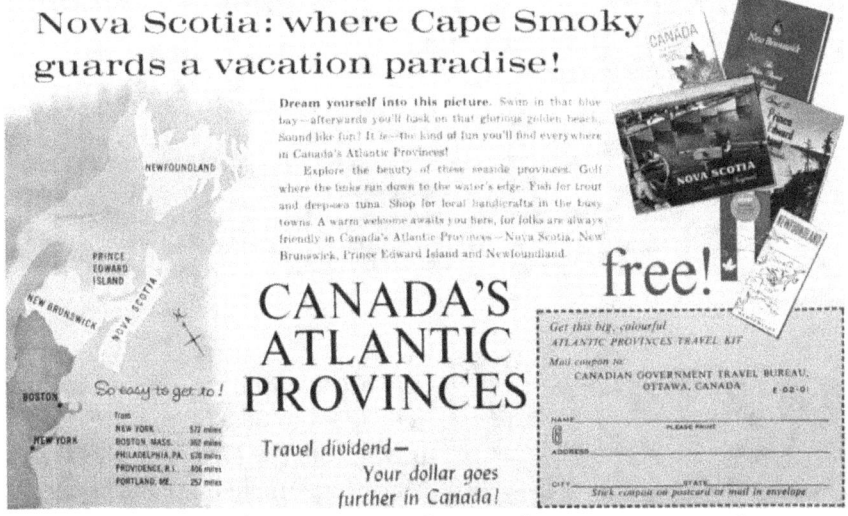

Nova Scotia: where Cape Smoky guards a vacation paradise!

Dream yourself into this picture. Swim in that blue bay—afterwards you'll bask on that glorious golden beach. Sound like fun? It *is*—the kind of fun you'll find everywhere in Canada's Atlantic Provinces!

Explore the beauty of these seaside provinces. Golf where the links run down to the water's edge. Fish for trout and deep-sea tuna. Shop for local handicrafts in the busy towns. A warm welcome awaits you here, for folks are always friendly in Canada's Atlantic Provinces—Nova Scotia, New Brunswick, Prince Edward Island and Newfoundland.

Canada's Atlantic Provinces
Travel dividend—Your dollar goes further in Canada!

President Kennedy Assassinated   22nd November 1963

On 22nd Nov 1963, J.F. Kennedy's leisurely motorcade through the streets of Dallas, Texas, was fatally interrupted by an assassin's gunfire. Kennedy, slumped in his wife's arms, was rushed to Parkland Memorial Hospital. The 35th President of the United States was pronounced dead 30 minutes after the shooting. He would be the fourth US President to die by assassination.

President Kennedy with his wife Jacqueline arrive at Dallas Love Field airport on the morning of 22nd November.

The motorcade provided maximum exposure for the press and local crowds. The Kennedy's traveled in the same limousine as Texas Governor John Connally and his wife Nellie. Vice President Johnson and his wife were two cars behind.

Below: The motorcade on Main Street near Delaney Plaza.

The presidential motorcade was scheduled to take 55 minutes to travel from the airport to the Trade Mart for a luncheon. Passing through Downtown Dallas, the motorcade entered Delaney Plaza at 12.30pm when the shooting took place. Assassin Lee Harvey Oswald fired three bullets from the 6th floor window of a nearby building. Kennedy was hit by two bullets in the neck and back of head. Connally was shot through his back, rib and chest. He received surgery and survived.

Over the next hour, as America and the world learned of the attack, police discovered Oswald's rifle and spent bullet casings on the 6th floor of the Texas School Book Depository building. Policeman J.D. Tippet soon spotted Oswald, becoming the second victim when Oswald shot and killed him. Witnesses led police to the Texas Theatre where Oswald was arrested.

That evening, Oswald was charged with the murders of Kennedy and Tippet. He denied the charges.

Two days later, as Oswald was being escorted to a car in the basement of the Dallas Police headquarters, distraught night club owner Jack Ruby fired a weapon at close range, killing the assassin. The shooting was broadcast live on American TV.

Top left: President Kennedy's casket transferred to Air Force One at Love Field airport, 22nd Nov 1963.

Right from top: Lyndon B. Johnson takes the oath of office aboard Air Force One. Jackie Kennedy, still in her blood-soaked clothes, looks on, 22nd Nov 1963.

Kennedy's family leaves Capitol after the funeral ceremony, 24th Nov 1963.

President Kennedy lying in state in the Capitol Rotunda, 24th-25th Nov 1963.

Jack Ruby takes aim at Oswald, 24th Nov 1963.

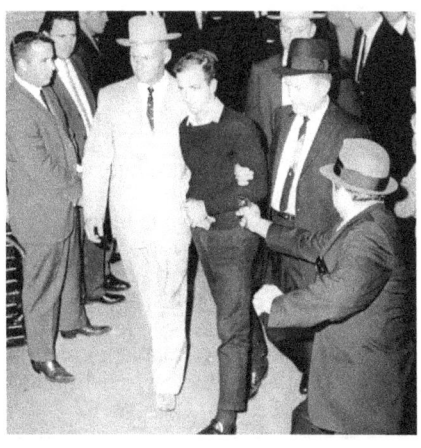

Advertisement

High school graduates: Your Country Needs You

Graduation's coming. *Now* is the time to think ahead. So think about this: your future is only as secure as your Country's.

In today's world, your home and your family are safe only as long as free nations are alert. This is why the U.S. Army needs men. Good men. Right now, the need for high school graduates is great. Are you ready to serve your Country?

Have a serious talk with your Army recruiter. Let him tell you the choices you have... the skills you can learn... the travel that awaits you. You'll get an idea of what it takes to feel like a man... and to act like one in your Country's behalf.

Remember, in these crucial times your future is only as secure as your Country's. See your local U.S. Army recruiter soon.

Cold War-Nuclear Arms Race

Cold War tensions between the two former allies—the USSR and the USA—had been increasing since the end of the war in 1945. Starting in the USA as policies for communist containment, the distrust and misunderstanding between the two sides quickly escalated from political squabbling to a military nuclear arms race. Trillions of dollars in military spending saw both sides stockpile their nuclear arsenals, strategically positioning their missiles closer and closer to each other.

In the early '60s the USA's global nuclear weapon stockpiles increased rapidly, peaking in 1967. By 1963, the USA had 28,133 nuclear weapons, against the Soviet's 4,238 weapons. Additionally, the UK held 394 weapons.[1]

Operation Dominic Swordfish, Pacific Ocean, 11th May 1952.

The nuclear arms race gave the two superpowers the pretext needed to test nuclear bombs on a massive scale. 1962 saw an astonishing 175 nuclear bomb tests carried out by the two superpowers, more than double the annual Cold War average.[2] The same year, the Cuban Missile Crisis brought the world to the brink of full-scale nuclear war, forcing the leaders of both sides into a dialog aimed to reduce political tensions.

Ten months later, on 5th Aug 1963, the Limited Test Ban Treaty was signed by representatives from the Soviet Union, USA and UK. Underground testing would still be permitted, but underwater, atmospheric and outer space testing would be halted. An additional 133 nations have signed since 1963.

President Kennedy signing the ratified Treaty at the White House, 7th Oct 1953.

[1] tandfonline.com/doi/pdf/10.2968/066004008.
[2] armscontrol.org/factsheets/nucleartesttally.

Cold War–Space Race

Throughout the 1960s, the Cold War dominated our lives on the ground and in the skies. Cold War tensions affected everything from our politics and education, to our interests in fashion and popular culture. By 1963, the USSR had achieved many firsts in the Space Race, putting them at a military, technological and intellectual advantage.

Yuri Gagarin became the first human in space, circling the earth in a 108-minute orbital flight on 12th Apr 1961. The Russian's success came as a huge blow to the Americans, who had hoped to be the first to send a man to space.

NASA's first full orbit of earth with a man on board occurred on 20th Feb 1962, nearly a full year behind the Soviets. Astronaut John Glenn made three Earth orbits.

Cosmonaut Valentina Tereshkova became the first woman in space on 16th June 1963, orbiting the earth 48 times on a 3-day solo mission. She remains the only woman to have made a solo space mission. On 22nd June, she was awarded the Hero of the Soviet Union medal and decorated with the Order of Lenin—the USSR's highest civilian honor.

Throughout the decade the Soviets continued to lead the Space Race with longer space flights, more complex space walks and challenging technical activities performed while in orbit. Ultimately the USA would achieve its goal, winning the Space Race in 1969 when Neil Armstrong and Edwin "Buzz" Aldrin landed, planted the American flag, and walked on the moon for 2 hours 15 minutes.

Cold War-Battlefield Vietnam

Fearful that a "domino effect" would see an uncontained spread of communism across the world, the US committed to supporting South Vietnam, financially and militarily, during its 30-year-long bloody civil war against North Vietnam (the Viet Cong). At the same time, communist China and USSR were jointly aiding the Viet Cong's invasion southward. Vietnam had become a Cold War battlefield.

Under the leadership of President Kennedy, America's involvement in the Vietnam War (known in Vietnam as the American War) was officially limited to training South Vietnamese soldiers, and supplying military aircraft and heavy machinery. However, US Forces did secretly engage in attacks against the Viet Cong, with the President's authorization.

US Green Beret conducting training, 1961.

US aircraft had also been spraying lethal herbicides to defoliate the dense jungle vegetation where the Viet Cong were suspected of hiding. Known as *Operation Ranch Hand,* an estimated 400,000 people were killed or maimed due to herbicide exposure.

President Kennedy continued to refuse the deployment of US combat troops in Vietnam. However, under the leadership of President Johnson, US combat troops would begin arriving by the thousands.

In all, 2.7 million American soldiers served in Vietnam over the ten years to 1973. More than 58,000 Americans died in battle, in addition to the more than 3 million Vietnamese (civilians and soldiers from both sides of battle).[1]

[1] britannica.com/event/Vietnam-War.

Advertisement

Put your hand over this clock-radio...
and see how tiny it actually is.

Now put your hand on your night table–and see how little room this General Electric clock radio actually takes.

That's why this new model C-551 makes such a good Christmas gift. Ladies like the way it subtracts clutter from the bedside table–and *adds* a stylish accent.

Men admire this–plus the C-551's practical side: its *lighted clock face*. The pillow speaker jack. The automatic shutoff switch. The wake-to-music or buzzer feature. The fine sound. So...

Put this compact clock-radio on your night table in place of your bulky old-timer. Or put it on your desk. And, by all means, put it at the top of your gift list. In fact, why not do *all* your shopping at your General Electric radio dealer's.

Advertisement

Fun-savers for '63 ...from Kodak!

Dont spend your summer weekends— save them with an easy-to-use Kodak camera!

P.S. Ask your dealer to show you the newest Kodak Fun-saver— the **Kodak Instamatic** Camera with **Kodapak** Film Cartridge!

Fun-savers for '63... from Kodak!

Don't spend your summer weekends–save them with an easy-to-use Kodak camera!

Steadiness is built in! Unique new horizontal shape gives a firmer grip for sharper, clearer shots. Built-in flash. Camera, film, flash-bulbs, batteries, neck strap all included in Brownie Super 27 Outfit... less than $22.

Easy to carry, easy to use! Weighs less than 8 ounces, including built-in flash! No need to focus. Has simple exposure settings. Takes sharp, clear snapshots or slides from as close as 4 ft. New Brownie Starmite II Camera... less than $12.

Take beautiful slides automatically! Electric-eye meter sets lens opening, tells you when to use built-in pop-up flash. Automatic flash exposure, too. Kodak Automatic 35F Camera... less than $100.

Automatic movies! No need to focus or set exposure. Electric eye, fast $f/1.6$ lens. Built-in filter, optical viewfinder. Kodak Automatic 8 Movie Camera... less than $55.

Be prepared for fun–with plenty of Kodak Film! You can *depend* on the name Kodak.

P.S. Ask your dealer to show you the newest Kodak Fun-Saver– The Kodak Instamatic Camera with Kodapak Film Cartridge!

The Summer of Our Discontent

Civil rights protests had been gaining momentum since the mid-'50s, with pro-segregation Alabama regularly at the center of campaigns. On 2nd May 1963, organizers in Birmingham, Alabama, boldly implemented the "Children's Crusade". Thousands of African American high-schoolers skipped school, many of them marching from the 16th Street Baptist Church towards City Hall. They were arrested and jailed.

The next day hundreds more marched again. This time they were violently attacked by police, dogs and water cannon, all broadcast to a shocked nation live on TV.

As the marches continued, President Kennedy intervened to negotiate an end to the protests. The *Birmingham Truce Agreement* (10th May) was seen as a victory for civil rights. White segregationists reacted with violence and bombings. Chaos resulted as thousands rioted in the streets and numerous buildings burned.

The bravery of the Birmingham children reinvigorated the civil rights movement nationwide. Sit-ins, marches and protests erupted in more than 100 cities. Riots and violent clashes broke out in New Orleans, Mississippi, Louisiana, Georgia, California, Virginia, the Carolinas, Florida, Massachusetts, and elsewhere. Police brutality was commonplace, as was the involvement of the Ku Klux Klan.

Above: Police attack children with water hoses and lead them to custody, 2nd-3rd May, 1963.

Martin Luther King Jnr. leads the Walk for Freedom in Detroit, Michigan, 23rd June 1963.

On 15th Sept, Ku Klux Klan members bombed the 16th Street Baptist Church, killing four African American girls.

Wallace at the University of Alabama (above) blocks entry to students James Alexander Hood and Vivian Malone (below).

President Kennedy broadcast from the Resolute desk in the Oval Office, 11th June 1963.

Alabama's governor George Wallace Jnr. maintained his inaugural speech pledge: "segregation now, segregation tomorrow, segregation forever". A staunch supporter of Jim Crow laws, with ties to the Ku Klux Klan, Wallace is best remembered for personally blocking two African American students from entering the University of Alabama on 11th June 1963. Known as the "Stand in the Schoolhouse Door", Wallace, flanked by Alabama National Guardsmen, was commanded to step aside by Federal Marshalls sent by President Kennedy.

Later that day, Kennedy federalized the Alabama National Guard under the Insurrection Act of 1807.

At 8pm, the President delivered a televised speech from the Oval Office expressing his support of the Civil Rights movement, which paved the way for the Civil Rights Act of 1964.

Described by Martin Luther King Jnr. as "the summer of our discontent", leaders of various civil rights groups, labor unions, church and student organizations, came together to plan a massive march on Washington. President Kennedy met with the leaders and, unable to cancel the march, arranged for his brother, Attorney General Robert Kennedy, to join the planning committee. The Kennedys were determined that the march would be a success and would be peaceful.

March on Washington   28th August 1963

More than 200,000 joined the March on Washington for Jobs and Freedom. Their demands included the creation of a comprehensive Civil Rights Bill, protection of the right to vote, unemployed worker training programs, minimum wages for workers, a Federal Act banning discrimination in hiring, and desegregation of all public schools.

Hollywood celebrities and popular vocalists entertained the crowd between the presentations of prominent speakers. The evening culminated in a rousing closing speech by Martin Luther King Jnr., which became known as the "I Have a Dream" speech.

The demand for change continued to build momentum, resulting in the Civil Rights Act of 1964 and the Voting Rights Act of 1965.

Right top and middle: The March on Washington crowd seen from the Lincoln Monument.

Right bottom: President Kennedy and Lyndon Johnson meet with the leaders of the March on Washington in the Oval Office, 28th Aug 1963, in the evening.

Below: Martin Luther King Jnr. delivers his "I Have a Dream" speech from the steps of the Lincoln Memorial.

Advertisement

The Caribbean, *wherever* you want to go: Pan Am – and only Pan Am – offers you the 14 favorite islands!

Wherever in the world you travel you're better off with Pan Am — world's most experienced airline!

(See your Pan Am Travel Agent)

The Caribbean, *whenever* you want to go: Pan Am offers you twice as many Jet flights as any other airline!

The Caribbean, *wherever* you want to go: Pan Am–and only Pan Am–offers you the 14 favorite islands!

The Caribbean, *whenever* you want to go: Pan Am offers you twice as many Jet flights as any other airline!

Life Sentence for Mandela

9th Oct '63 – 12th Jun '64

President Nelson Mandela, Oct 1994.

During the 1940s and '50s, South African lawyer and anti-Apartheid activist Nelson Mandela rose through the ranks of the African National Congress (ANC). With the aim of ending the ruling National Party's system of Apartheid, white supremacy and racial segregation, Mandela co-founded and led the new military arm of the ANC–uMkhonto we Sizwe (MK). The Nationals immediately outlawed the ANC and MK.

Mandela had become known as "the Black Pimpernel" for his ability to evade police. He spent months traveling across South Africa disguised as a chauffeur, organizing anti-government activities. Late in 1962, Mandela was finally captured, tried, and found guilty of inciting workers to strike and leaving the country without permission. He was sentenced to five years in prison.

Mandela casting his vote in the 1994 elections. It was the first time Mandela had voted in his life.

On 9th October 1963, a new trial began against eleven leaders of the ANC, MK and the Communist Party. Known as the Rivonia Trial, all were given life sentences, including Mandela who was still behind bars at the time. Most would serve decades as political prisoners. Mandela was released in 1990, after 27 years in detention.

Nelson Mandela would become the first black President of South Africa in 1994, following the country's first fully democratic election.

Advertisement

Public phones are found in the likeliest places!

Public phones are handy everywhere. We put them on streets and highways, corners and crossings, in parks, stores, stations, lobbies, terminals—wherever they're needed. They can save time, help you make dates, chat with friends, find directions, get aid in a hurry. So look for them, and use them as you use your phones at home.

 Bell Telephone System

Public phones are found in the likeliest places!

Public phones are handy everywhere. We put them on streets and highways, corners and crossings, in parks, stores, stations, lobbies, terminals–wherever they're needed. They can save time, help you make dates, chat with friends, find directions, get aid in a hurry. So look for them, and use them as you use your phones at home.

The Profumo Crisis

In May 1963, John Profumo, British Secretary of State for War, found himself at the center of the biggest scandal in British political history. He had earlier lied to the House of Commons, denying an affair he had had two years earlier with the then 19-year-old showgirl Christine Keeler. Keeler had been simultaneously having an affair with Soviet naval attaché Captain Yevgeny Ivanov, creating a serious national security risk during the height of the Cold War.

Left to right: John Profumo, Christine Keeler and Captain Yevgeny Ivanov.

British Intelligence MI5 had kept close watch on the three, knowing that Ivanov was a Soviet intelligence agent, and that Keeler might be useful as a "honey trap" to secure his defection. Profumo's interest in Keeler complicated the plan.

As gossip circulated, Soviet Intelligence recalled Ivanov. Keeler tried to sell her story to the press, forcing Profumo to categorically deny any "impropriety whatsoever in [his] acquaintanceship with Miss Keeler." On 31st May, a guilt ridden Profumo confessed to his wife and to Prime Minister Macmillan, handing in his resignation.

The person connecting the three was socialite Stephen Ward. When Ward was charged with procuring women under 21 to have sex with other persons, namely politicians, the British press speculated widely. The credibility of the ruling Conservative Government was severely damaged, resulting in the resignation of the Prime Minister, and the defeat of the Conservatives at the next election.

On 3rd August '63, Ward committed suicide by barbiturate poisoning. Evidence has since shown Ward was a political scapegoat, and not at all the deviant he was portrayed to be.

The Great Train Robbery   8th August 1963

It would become known as the "heist of the century"—the meticulously executed robbery of a Royal Mail train traveling from Glasgow, Scotland to London, England. Fifteen robbers boarded the night train and looted 120 sacks of mail containing £2.6 million ($3 million USD, equivalent to $29 million USD today). With insider information on the train's schedule and cargo, the robbers tricked the train driver to stop.

They uncoupled the first two carriages, containing the high-value packages, from the rest, moving them to Bridego Bridge where their get-away vehicle was waiting. The gang formed a human chain to offload the mail sacks.

Scene from the miniseries *The Great Train Robbery* (BBC. 2013).

Police were quick to find the abandoned hideout and identified most of the gang members from fingerprints left behind. Twelve of the robbers were later caught, tried, and imprisoned. The bulk of the money, consisting of £1 and £5 bills, was soon spent and never recovered.

The Great Train Robbery has given rise to countless books, films and television shows. Several of the gang have become infamous for their daring prison escapes and years on the run. Many rebuilt their lives abroad after prison release.

Ronnie Biggs, the most infamous of the gang, escaped after serving only 15 months behind bars. Fleeing to Paris, he underwent plastic surgery, acquired new identity papers, moved to Australia and from there to Brazil. He spent 37 years on the run, returning to the UK in 2001. He was arrested upon his return.

Ronnie Biggs mug shot in 1964.

Advertisement

LUCKY DOG

The Honda's a doll. Push the button and you're in business, with never a complaint from her willing 4-stroke 50cc OHV engine.

At 45 mph you're riding on silk.

The biggest draw is her figure—a trim $245 plus the customary set-up charge. She doesn't gulp gas. Just sips it—225 miles to a gallon. She has 3-speed transmission, automatic clutch, dual cam-type brakes on both wheels. Even an optional electric starter.

Now you know why so many guys like running around with a Honda. Lots of fun for very little money. A real swinger.

Lucky dog.

For address of your nearest dealer or other information, write: American Honda Motor Co., Inc., Department E, 100 West Alondra, Gardena, California.

HONDA

World's biggest seller!

Who Were The Rat Pack?

They were known as The Rat Pack—a group of entertainer friends, who sang together, acted together, played hard and drank harder together. They had links to politicians, mafia, and Hollywood elite. In the early '60s, their favorite hangout was The Sands Hotel in Las Vegas, and between them, they transformed this dusty, desert town into the glamorous gambling and entertainment capitol of the world.

At its core, the Pack comprised: Frank Sinatra, Dean Martin, Sammy Davis Jnr, Peter Lawford and Joey Bishop. Their shows were broadcast on live TV, enticing other celebrities to perform in Las Vegas, and turning the place into a tourist destination town.

The Rat Pack were the kings of cool. They had swag, talent, energy, money and power. To see the Rat Pack at the Sands, a show with dinner and two drinks, cost a cool $5.95 per person.

At their peak, The Rat Pack made 5 films together including *Ocean's 11* (Warner Bros. 1960), *Sergeants Three* (United Artists, 1962), and *Four for Texas* (Warner Bros. 1963).

Below Left: Martin, Judy Garland and Sinatra.
Below Right: Sinatra, the leader of The Pack, recorded 14 albums during the years 1961-'63.

1963 in Cinema and Film

From its peak in the mid-1940s, cinema attendance faced a steady decline as TV sets took pride of place in our living rooms. Cinemas struggled to stay profitable and by 1963 many had been forced to close. The motion picture industry needed creative ways to maintain strong ticket sales.

In order to win over new audiences, movie studios targeted younger viewers who had more leisure time and cash to spare. Comedies proved to be box office favorites, with eight of the top ten highest grossing films of the year being comedies.

A young Anne Margaret as Kim MacAfee, dancing with her peers in *Bye Bye Birdie*.

Jackie Chan, circa 1970.

Highest Paid Stars

1	Doris Day	5	Cary Grant
2	John Wayne	6	Elizabeth Taylor
3	Rock Hudson	7	Elvis Presley
4	Jack Lemmon	8	Sandra Dee

1963 film debuts

Jackie Chan	Big and Little Wong Tin
Robert Duvall	To Kill a Mockingbird
Sally Field	Moon Pilot
Sydney Pollack	War Hunt
Bernardo Bertolucci	The Grim Reaper

* From en.wikipedia.org/wiki/1963_in_film.

Top Grossing Films of the Year

1	Cleopatra	20th Century Fox	$26,000,000
2	How the West Was Won	MGM	$20,932,883
3	It's a Mad, Mad, Mad, Mad World	United Artists	$20,800,000
4	Tom Jones	United Artists	$17,070,000
5	Irma la Douce	United Artists/Mirisch	$11,921,784
6	Son of Flubber	Walt Disney/Buena Vista	$9,100,000
7	Charade	Universal Pictures	$6,363,000
8	Bye Bye Birdie	Columbia Pictures	$6,200,000
9	Come Blow Your Horn	Paramount Pictures	$6,000,000
=	Move Over, Darling	20th Century Fox	$6,000,000
10	The Great Escape	United Artists/Mirisch	$5,546,000

* From en.wikipedia.org/wiki/1963_in_film by box office gross in the USA.

The romantic comedy *Irma la Douce* cast Shirley MacLaine to replace Marilyn Monroe following Monroe's death in 1962.

It's a Mad, Mad, Mad, Mad World boasted an all-star cast of comedians including Spencer Tracy, Milton Berle, Ethel Merman, Mickey Rooney, and Jimmy Durante.

A Decade of Cinema Epics

The 1960s saw cinema studios take big risks with extravagant and spectacular epic films. Exotic locations, expensive sets, multiple A-list actors and casts of thousands ensured big ticket sales at the box office.

The early '60s in cinema was memorable for many sweeping heroic period films such as *Spartacus* (1960), *Lawrence of Arabia* (1962) and the costliest epic of them all–David Lean's *Cleopatra* (1963).

Cleopatra arrives in Rome atop a black marble sphinx, pulled by an army of slaves.

Requiring $44 million to make (a substantial blow-out from the original $4 million budget), *Cleopatra* is legendary for the off-screen drama and chaos which contributed to the out-of-control costs.

Taylor and Burton in Cleopatra.

Actress Elizabeth Taylor secured a record-setting $1 million to star in the film. The star would ultimately earn $7 million in salary and percentage of gross earnings.

Rex Harrison (Julius Caesar), and on-screen off-screen love interest Richard Burton (Mark Antony) complete the movie's love triangle.

Although both married at the time, Taylor and Burton's illicit and scandalous affair was not discrete, providing the film studio with negative (but free) publicity.

Troubles began early during filming, when Taylor contracted meningitis and needed time off set. She later developed a serious bout of pneumonia requiring an emergency tracheotomy. Already over budget, filming at London's Pinewood Studios shut down. The lavish sets were dismantled as the entire production moved to the warmer climate of Rome's Cinecittà to better protect Taylor's health from the damp British winter.

At the same time, the film's director was changed, and both the original leading men dropped, to be replaced by Harrison and Burton. All usable footage was discarded as the new director demanded a script rewrite. Numerous writers attempted to devise a workable script, wasting more valuable time.

Burton as Antony, Harrison as Caesar, and Taylor as Cleopatra.

Costs escalated with the requirement for 79 detailed and enormous production sets, and up to 10,000 extras. An unprecedented 26,000 costumes were created. Taylor alone required 65 costumes, including one gown made from 24-carat gold cloth.

As the budget skyrocketed to more than $320 million in today's terms, 20th Century Fox sold nearly 300 acres of its Los Angeles back lot. Cleopatra remains one of the most expensive films in cinema history. The film finally recouped its costs years later, with sales of television rights.

Taylor wearing a gold winged costume.

Advertisement

General Electric's new 6-speaker coffee table...

for people who like stereo

GENERAL ELECTRIC

General Electric's new 6-speaker coffee table... for people who like stereo ...and appreciate fine furniture.

General Electric fashions *The Wellington* of solid hardwood, finished in genuine maple veneer. (Also in contemporary walnut.)

Notice how usable the tabletop is. The hidden control panel takes only a fraction of the $55^1/_2$" length. The rest is all yours. The hardwood surface is treated to shrug off spills, abuse. You enjoy this vast sweep of table thanks to...

"Swingaway" turntable—an innovation offered only by General Electric. Swing it out, load the Garrard changer with a stack of records, swing it away—out of sight.

This instrument produces superb stereophonic sound. Each channel has an 8" woofer, beamed downward; plus a pair of 4" tweeters, aimed front and back. Result: you are surrounded by high-fidelity stereo sound. You may also amplify the bass for background effect.

An AM/FM/FM-Stereo radio is optional. You also have the option to include General Electric's unique Home Music Distribution System: a tiny transmitter in the console sends radio or recorded music through your household wiring. Hear it in any room by simply plugging in the portable receiver-speaker.

See the many innovations in stereo, available only from your G-E dealer.

Musical Memories

American style rock 'n' roll had ruled the 1950s and early '60s, with movies, television, fashion, youth culture and attitudes worldwide influenced by this American export. However, British home-grown rock artists were developing their own unique interpretation of the rock genre. By 1963, music critics and youth worldwide began to take notice. The mid-'60's demand for all things British–known as the "British Invasion"–made The Beatles, Cliff Richard, The Kinks, The Who, The Rolling Stones, The Yardbirds, and others, household names.

11th Feb– The Beatles recorded ten songs for their first LP, *Please Please Me*. This, and the ten albums to follow, all reached #1 in the UK, as did 17 of their singles released during the '60s. As their popularity exploded, the frenzied enthusiasm of hoards of screaming fans, became known as "Beatlemania".

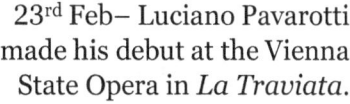

23rd Feb– Luciano Pavarotti made his debut at the Vienna State Opera in *La Traviata*.

5th March– Country music stars Patsy Cline, Cowboy Copas, and Hawkshaw Hawkins were killed, along with their pilot, in small plane crash in Tennessee.

7th June– The Rolling Stones released their first single, a cover version of Chuck Berry's *Come On*. They continued to record covers and perform as support act to various artists for most of '63-'64, before finding their stride in 1965.

1963 Billboard Top 30 Songs

	Artist	Song Title
1	The Beach Boys	Surfin' U.S.A.
2	Skeeter Davis	The End of the World
3	The Cascades	Rhythm of the Rain
4	The Chiffons	He's So Fine
5	Bobby Vinton	Blue Velvet
6	Paul & Paula	Hey Paula
7	Little Stevie Wonder	Fingertips
8	Andy Williams	Can't Get Used to Losing You
9	The Angels	My Boyfriend's Back
10	Kyu Sakamoto	Sukiyaki

The Beach Boys, 1963.

Paul and Paula, 1963.

Andy Williams, 1963.

	Artist	Song Title
11	The Tymes	So Much in Love
12	Peter, Paul & Mary	Puff, the Magic Dragon
13	Peter, Paul & Mary	Blowin' in the Wind
14	The Surfaris	Wipe Out
15	Al Martino	I Love You Because
16	The Rebels	Wild Weekend
17	Bobby Darin	You're the Reason I'm Living
18	The Four Seasons	Walk Like a Man
19	Inez & Charlie Foxx	Mockingbird
20	Little Peggy March	I Will Follow Him

Peter, Paul and Mary, 1963.

Lesley Gore, 1967.

21	The Chantays	Pipeline
22	Jan & Dean	Surf City
23	Lesley Gore	It's My Party
24	Eydie Gormé	Blame It on the Bossa Nova
25	The Dovells	You Can't Sit Down
26	Martha and the Vandellas	Heat Wave
27	Randy & the Rainbows	Denise
28	The Rooftop Singers	Walk Right In
29	Jimmy Soul	If You Wanna Be Happy
30	Trini Lopez	If I Had a Hammer

* From the *Billboard* top 30 singles of 1963.

Advertisement

Dresses from the *National Bellas Hess* Home Shopping Catalog, Summer 1963.

Fashion Trends of the 1960s

The 1960s was a decade of fashion extremes driven by a vibrant and vocal youth, shifting social movements, rebelliousness and rejection of traditions. It was an exciting decade for fashion, with new trends that caught on and shifted quickly.

In the early '60s, fashion was content to continue the conservative classic style of the previous decade. The elegant sheath dress and tailored skirt-suits were still favored for day wear. And no lady would dare to venture out without her full ensemble of matching accessories. Gloves, hat, scarf, jewelry and stiletto or kitten-heel shoes were mandatory for any outing.

Christian Dior's voluptuous "New Look", favored throughout the 1950s, was still popular for cocktails or dinners. Less formal than the stiffer '50s styles, dresses retained their hour-glass shape but were now made with softer patterned fabrics. Skirts stayed long, full and very lady-like.

Television, cinema and magazine coverage kept us abreast of the latest in haute couture and street style, inspiring us with our favorite fashion icons.

Jacqueline Kennedy may have been the US first lady for only three years, but as first lady of fashion, her iconic status has endured till this day.

Jacqueline Kennedy, wearing her signature pearl necklace.

Always impeccably groomed, with perfectly applied make-up and coiffured hair, here are a few of her iconic looks:

- Tailored skirt-suit with three-quarter-sleeve box jacket and pill box hat in matching fabric.
- Sheath dress with low-heeled pump shoes and three-quarter gloves.
- A-line dress, long or short, with long gloves for evening.

After more than a decade of adherence to Dior's New Look, the first rumblings of change were being felt from Europe. The fashion houses of Italy were enticing us with bold new shapes and modern textiles.

Elastic jersey pants with laminated silk shirt by Emilio Schuberth. Layered form dress by Cesare Guidi.

Advertisement

Just like drying your hair in the fresh desert air!

The new Schick *Le Salon* professional hairdryer especially designed for home use

(gives you the ultimate in speed and comfort!)

Le Salon by Schick dries your hair faster, better than any other you've ever used. Its soft, zephyr-like air flows from tiny holes in the roomy hood... air so gentle you never need a net. And so comfortable! With Le Salon you can forget about covering your ears or neck. No nerve-wracking noise either. And so safe to use–doesn't change the color of our bleached or tinted hair the way other hairdryers can. (Perfect for children's hair, too!) With Le Salon, you have easy-to-adjust temperature control. And you'll love how it fits into any decor, moves easily on its own wheels, stores in the smallest space.

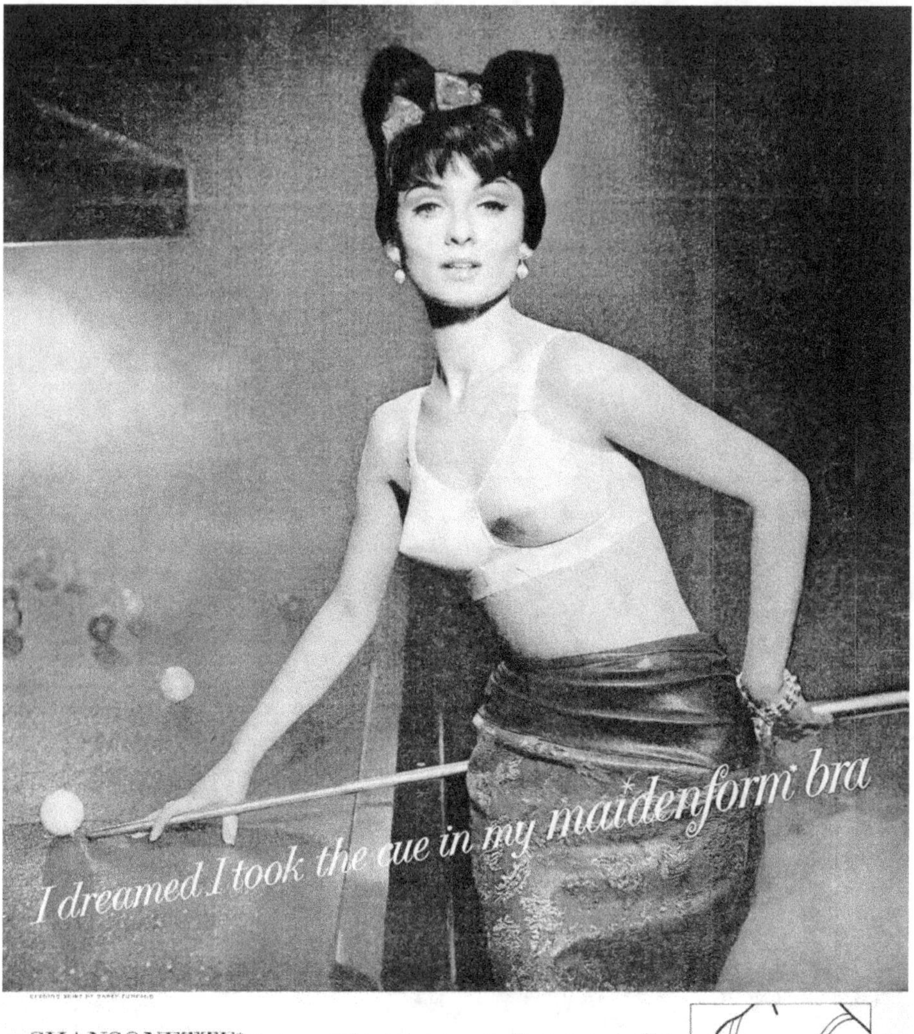

Advertisement

CHANSONETTE* shapes and supports your figure naturally

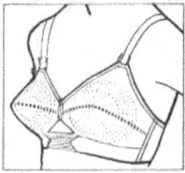

2.00

I dreamed I took the cue in my Maidenform bra

Chansonette shapes and supports your figure <u>naturally</u>

Special stitching in the cups is what does it. Firming circles give you extra support and uplift–spoke-stitching fully accentuates your curves. Below the cups, a snug 'uplift' band holds the bra securely, comfortably, all day. Elastic insert 'breathes' whenever you do! Take the cue—wear Chansonette! White or black all cotton broadcloth–A, B, C cups. Also available in "Dacron" polyester & cotton, 2.50; Lace, 3.50; all-elastic back, 3.00; Contour, 3.00; Full-Length, 3.50.

The decade of the 1960s would belong to the British youth centered around London, who would soon capture the world's attention with their free spirits, energy, music, and style. The "British Invasion" exploded onto the world in the early '60s, introducing us to the "Mods", and later to the "Swinging Sixties". These movements defined the era and changed the world of fashion forever.

The Mods were clean-cut college boys who favored slim-fitting suits or short jackets over turtle-neck or buttoned up polo shirts. Pants were pipe-legged with no cuffs, worn over pointed polished shoes or ankle boots. Mods were obsessed with Italian fashion, French haircuts, and alternative music.

For the girls, London designer Mary Quant created fashion for the young and free-spirited woman. Quant invented the mini skirt, worn with bold colored or patterned tights. Her boutique featured simple short dresses in bold or floral patterns. By the mid-'60s she championed hot pants for women.

Mary Quant's experimental use of new materials was revolutionary. She created synthetic dresses, patent plastic boots, shiny PVC raincoats and bold, colorful jewelry, handbags and accessories.

By the mid-'60s the world would be captivated by the unstoppable energy of London's Swinging Sixties. The term captured the modern fun-loving hedonism of swinging London. It was the era of the British supermodel–tall, skinny, leggy young ladies, with enormous eyes and descriptive names. Jean Shrimpton, Twiggy, and Penelope Tree were in-demand icons world-wide. The British supermodels broke with the aristocratic look of earlier-generation models, redefining beauty standards for a younger, more care-free generation.

Penelope Tree for *Vogue*, October 1967.

Twiggy for *Italian Vogue*, July 1967.

Twiggy various photo shoots.

Jean Shrimpton for *Australian Women's Weekly*, August 1965.

As the fashion and attitudes of swinging London spread to America and other parts of the world, the sub-culture became commercialized on a mass scale and began to loose its vitality. The Swinging Sixties morphed into the psychedelic rock and early hippie movements.

Led by musicians such as The Beatles, The Beach Boys, Pink Floyd and The Who, and fuelled by the widespread use of marijuana and LSD, psychedelic fashion became an expression of the hallucinogenic experience with bright colors, swirling patterns and kaleidoscopic floral designs.

From The Beatles *Magical Mystery Tour,* 1967.

The psychedelic rock movement petered out by the end of the 1960s, but the hippie generation was only just beginning. Hippies would drive fashion forward, well into the next decade.

Advertisement

Testing... Testing...

That busy airplane above is the brilliant new Boeing 727, America's first short-range jetliner. It's engaged in the most intensive test program in airliner history. During the rest of this year, four 727s will be put through exhaustive flight tests. You'll be able to fly aboard this magnificent new Boeing jet beginning early next year. You'll find the cabin roomy and luxurious; the ride, incredibly quiet and smooth. The 727 can operate from 5000-foot runways, bringing the advantages of jet travel to hundreds of smaller cities. These airlines have already ordered 131 Boeing 727s: American, Ansett-ANA, Eastern, Lufthansa, Trans-Australia, TWA and United.

Boeing 727

Technology and Medicine

30th Jan– Ivan Sutherland exhibited his Sketchpad program, a forerunner to modern computer-aided design programs.

9th Feb– Boeing conducted its first flight for the new 727 jet. The 727 would remain in production for 21 years

18th Apr– Dr James Campbell performed the first successful nerve transplant from one person to another.

18th Nov– Bell Telephone introduced the Touch-Tone telephone, the first push button phone.

7th Dec– The instant replay, invented by Tony Verna for CBS, was first used in a US Army vs Navy football game. When the replay finally worked during a live TV broadcast, the jubilant announcer proclaimed, "This is not live. Ladies and gentlemen, Army did not score again!"

1963– John Enders licensed his vaccine against the measles virus. Prior to widespread vaccination, measles caused an estimated 2.6 million deaths each year.

1963– Harvey Ross Ball designed the smiley face symbol for an advertising campaign. He earned $45 for the now iconic logo. Ball never applied for a trademark for his work.

Advertisement

What under the sun are these 73 beauties doing?

If it looks like they're cheering something, they are! It's the fact that Bulova makes 73 glamorous gold watch styles—a *different* one for each girl to time her tan by.

We have handsome gold watches for men, too. Lots of them! In fact, Bulova makes more kinds of watches, at a wider range of prices, than anybody else under the sun.

Not just *more* watches, but *better* watches. For instance, Bulova gold watches get an extra layer of precious gold at points of hardest wear—like the case edges and the stem-winder. And to protect the movement, Bulova insists on a minimum of 17 jewels—more durable than the hardest steel.

Persnickety? Sure we are! That's why you always get a gift-quality watch from Bulova. One you can give or wear with pride, because it's made with pride. Every Bulova is engineered by the same skilled craftsmen who created Accutron, the world's only electronic wrist timepiece.

When you think of a watch, think of Bulova. You'll get *more styles* to choose from, *more quality* for your money—from $25 to $2500. Your jeweler knows it's true—and he's America's watch expert. See him soon.

When you think of a watch—think of Bulova. The Gift-Quality Watch

Also in Sports

19th Jan– Roy Emerson won the 1st of 5 straight Australian titles at the Australian Championships Men's Tennis beating fellow Australian Ken Fletcher 6-3, 6-3, 6-1.

20th Feb– Willie Mays became the highest-paid player in MLB when he signed a $100,000 contract with the San Francisco Giants.

Seven days later Mickey Mantle would sign for the same amount with the NY Yankees.

7th Apr– 23-year-old Jack Nicklaus won the first of his record 6 Green Jackets at the US Masters Tournament Augusta National.

1st May– The Gillette Cup held the world's first one-day cricket competition between English county teams at Old Trafford, UK. In 1971 the rules were adopted for the world's first international one-day cricket match between England and Australia, at the MCG in Australia.

14th Jul– French cyclist Jacques Anquetil won his 4th Tour de France, (1957, 1961-1963). He would win again in 1964, making 4 consecutive wins and becoming the first rider to win 5 times.

7th Sep– The Pro Football Hall of Fame opened in Canton, Ohio with 17 inductees in the charter class.

Other News from 1963

22ⁿᵈ Jan– French President Charles de Gaulle and German Federal Chancellor Konrad Adenauer signed the Élysée Treaty, a treaty of friendship and co-operation between France and West Germany.

6ᵗʰ Feb-27ᵗʰ Mar– Her Majesty Queen Elizabeth II and the Duke of Edinburgh made a 7-week tour of New Zealand and Australia. They would use the Royal Yacht Britannia as their base for daily tours and to entertain dignitaries.

7ᵗʰ Mar– Separatist guerrilla group Front de Libération du Québec (FLC) began their bombing campaign with the goal of establishing an independent and socialist Quebec. They would engage in 160 violent attacks over an 8-year period.

21ˢᵗ Mar– The Alcatraz Island federal penitentiary in San Francisco Bay was permanently closed after 29 years of operation. The prison was deemed too expensive to run.

7ᵗʰ Apr– President Tito was proclaimed President for Life under Yugoslavia's new constitution. He ruled until his death in 1980.

10ᵗʰ Apr– The submarine USS Tresher sank in the Atlantic with all men aboard. None of the men were recovered.

3rd Jun– Pope John XXIII, head of the Catholic Church, died at the Vatican triggering a conclave to elect a new pope. After six ballots of the papal conclave, Cardinal Montini of Milan was elected on 21st Jun, changing his name to Pope Paul VI.

26th Jul– A 6.1 magnitude earthquake hit Skopje, Yugoslavia, destroying 80% of the city. More than 200,000 people were left homeless, with at least 1,000 deaths.

16th Sep– The Federation of Malaysia was formed when Singapore, British North Borneo (Sabah) and Sarawak joined the eleven states of Malaya. Two years later Singapore would be expelled from the Federation, becoming a sovereign, independent nation.

30th Sep– Hurricane Flora destroyed thousands of homes and buildings throughout the Caribbean. More than 6,000 people were killed when the Category 5 hurricane, with winds exceeding 170 miles per hour, tore through Trinidad and Tobago, Haiti, Cuba, and Grenada,.

7th Nov– After 14 days trapped down a mine, eleven miners were rescued in what became known as West Germany's Wunder von Lengede (Miracle of Lengede).

8th Dec– Frank Sinatra, Jr. was kidnapped at Harrah's Lake Tahoe (Nevada). His famous father paid the $240,000 ransom to secure his release.

1963– The Coca-Cola Company created Tab cola, its first diet drink. The beverage was sweetened with a mixture of cyclamate and saccharin. Cyclamate was later removed due to safety concerns.

Advertisement

The perfect gift for Him

Now he can make permanent, professional labels in seconds! A turn of the dial, a squeeze of the hand... raised letters, numbers, symbols come out white on a colored background. The Dymo Home Labelmaker is available at fine stores everywhere for only $9.95.

The perfect gift for Her

Dymo raised-letter labels come in 15 colors (even home decorator shades)... have adhesive on the back so they stick to any smooth surface. White letters are easy to read, won't rub off. Dymo Home Labelmaker is available at fine stores everywhere for only $9.95.

Say it in Dymo... make your words stick!

Advertisement

Take the hopping out of shopping, let your fingers do the walking. A quick turn through the Yellow Pages tells you who sells what and where. Just look under Furniture, Electric Appliances, Lumber—or anything. Find it fast and easy when you **shop the Yellow Pages way!**

Famous People Born in 1963

14th Jan– Steven Soderbergh, American producer, director & writer.

16th Jan– James May, English TV presenter.

18th Jan– Tom Alexander, American writer, broadcaster, composer & voice actor.

19th Jan– Martin Bashir, British reporter & TV presenter.

26th Jan– Andrew Ridgeley, British songwriter, guitarist & producer (Wham).

17th Feb– Michael Jordan, American basketball player.

19th Feb– Seal [Henry Olusegun Adeola Samuel], British singer & songwriter.

21st Feb– Greg Turner, New Zealand golfer.

27th Mar– Quentin Tarantino, American director & screenwriter.

2nd Apr– Mike Gascoyne, British motor racing engineer, designer, writer & broadcaster.

4th Apr– Graham Norton [Walker], Irish comedian & TV presenter.

13th Apr– Gary Kasparov, Russian chess player (world champion 1985-93).

18th Apr– Conan Chris O'Brien, American TV host (Late Night).

26th Apr– Jet Li [Li Lianjie], Chinese Singaporean actor & martial artist.

25th May– Mike Myers, Canadian actor & comedian.

4th Jun– Mossimo Giannulli, American fashion designer.

9th Jun– Johnny Depp, American actor.

15th Jun– Helen Hunt, American actress.

25th Jun– George Michael [Georgios Kyriacos Panayiotou], English singer-songwriter (d. 2016).

30th Jul– Lisa Kudrow, American actress.

31st Jul– Fatboy Slim [Norman Cook], British musician & record producer.

9th Aug– Whitney Houston, American singer, actress & film producer (d. 2012).

21st Aug– Mohammed VI of Morocco, King of Morocco (1999-present).

1st Oct– Mark McGwire, American MLB 1st baseman & coach (12x All Star).

5th Oct– Laura Davies, British golfer (4 major titles).

6th Oct– Elisabeth Shue, American actress.

11th Oct– Faisal bin Al Hussein, Prince of Jordan, son of King Hussein & Princess Muna.

5th Nov– Tatum O'Neal, American actress.

10th Nov– Hugh Bonneville, English actor.

21st Nov– Nicollette Sheridan, British actress.

5th Dec– Eddie "the Eagle" Edwards, English ski jumper.

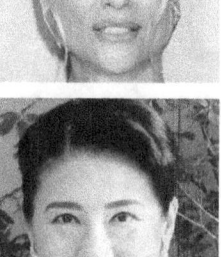

9th Dec– Empress Masako, Empress of Japan.

18th Dec– Brad Pitt, American actor & producer.

Advertisement

1963 in Numbers

Census Statistics [1]

- Population of the world — 3.21 billion
- Population in the United States — 194.93 million
- Population in the United Kingdom — 53.50 million
- Population in Canada — 18.94 million
- Population in Australia — 10.85 million
- Average age for marriage of women — 20.5 years old
- Average age for marriage of men — 22.8 years old
- Average family income USA — $6,200 per year
- Unemployment rate USA — 5.5 %

Costs of Goods [2]

- Average home — $19,785
- Average new car — $3,235
- A gallon of gasoline — $0.31
- Bananas — $0.59 per pound
- Peas, Green Giant — $0.19 per can
- Onions — $0.09 per pound
- Cheese, sharp cheddar — $0.65 per pound
- Beef, porterhouse steak — $0.89 per pound
- Bacon — $0.59 per pound
- SPAM — $0.39 per can
- Fresh Eggs — $0.45 per dozen
- Toothpaste, Crest extra large — $0.64 per tube
- Charcoal briquettes — $0.99 per 20 pounds
- Drive-in movie — $1.00 per car

1 Figures taken from worldometers.info/world-population, US National Center for Health Statistics, Divorce and Divorce Rates US (cdc.gov/nchs/data/series/sr_21/sr21_029.pdf) and United States Census Bureau, Historical Marital Status Tables (census.gov/data/tables/time-series/demo/families/marital.html).
2 Figures from thepeoplehistory.com, mclib.info/reference/local-history & dqydj.com/historical-home-prices/.

Advertisement

Put them together and dial anywhere

There are 475 parts in your Bell telephone. Fabricating many of the parts, then putting them all together, is Western Electric's job.

Behind the telephone is a surprising number of other communications products. Thousand of miles of telephone cable crisscross the nation underground. Crossing far-flung mountain ranges, complex microwave systems. And in thousands of telephone central offices, untold miles of wire, millions of switches, transistors and related equipment made by Western Electric—all this so you can reach any of the 68 million other Bell telephones across the land.

To help meet today's communications demands, Western Electric manufactures precision products that work compatibly and function faultlessly, each with each, as one dependable, integrated telephone network.

This takes teamwork. These parts must and do work together because Western Electric works together with the Bell Telephone Laboratories and the Bell telephone companies to bring you the best telephone service anywhere in the world. We work best because we work together.

Western Electric   Manufacturing and supply unit of the Bell System

Advertisement

Some Volkswagen owners look down on other Volkswagen owners.

Some Volkswagen owners look down on the other Volkswagen owners.

When you graduate from a Volkswagen Sedan to a Volkswagen Station Wagon, you really step up in the world.

The Station Wagon stands a good foot taller than other cars.

And it holds more than the biggest conventional wagon you can find.

But the VW Wagon isn't only tall. It's also short.

We saved 4 feet of hood in the front by putting the engine in the back.

Big as it is inside, it's only 9 inches longer than the Volkswagen Sedan.

So people who move up to the high-slung model still feel very much at home.

They park in the same little spots.

They still don't worry about freezing or boiling; the engine is air-cooled.

They still go a long way on a gallon of gas (about 24 miles) and a very long way on a set of tires (about 30,000 miles).

And it just tickles them to drive one Volkswagen and look down on a million others.

A heartfelt plea from the author:

I sincerely hope you enjoyed reading this book and that it brought back many fond memories from the past.

Success as an author has become increasingly difficult with the proliferation of **AI generated** copycat books by unscrupulous sellers. They are clever enough to escape copyright action and use dark web tactics to secure paid-for **fake reviews**, something I would never do.

Hence I would like to ask you—I plead with you—the reader, to leave a star rating or review on Amazon. This helps make my book discoverable for new readers, and helps me to compete fairly against the devious copycats.

If this book was a gift to you, you can leave stars or a review on your own Amazon account, or you can ask the gift-giver or a family member to do this on your behalf.

I have enjoyed researching and writing this book for you and would greatly appreciate your feedback.

Best regards,
Bernard Bradforsand-Tyler.

Please leave a
book review/rating at:

https://bit.ly/1963-reviews

Or scan the QR code:

Flashback books make the perfect gift- see the full range at

https://bit.ly/FlashbackSeries

Image Attributions

Photographs and images used in this book are reproduced courtesy of the following:

Page 6 – From *Life* Mag 6th Sep 1963. Source: books.google.com/books?id=blIEAAAAMBAJ&printsec (PD image).*
Page 8 – Detail of Frigidaire advertisement, from *Life* Magazine, 16th Aug 1963. Source: books.google.com/books?id= H1IEAAAAMBAJ&printsec (PD image).*
Page 9 – Detail of Western Auto advertisement, from Life Magazine, 16th Aug 1963. Source: books.google.com/books?id= H1IEAAAAMBAJ&printsec (PD image).*
Page 10 – From *Life* Mag 17th May 1963. Source: books.google.com/books?id=2kgEAAAAMBAJ&printsec (PD image).*
Page 11 – From *Life* Mag 12th Jul 1963. Source: books.google.com/books?id=K1IEAAAAMBAJ&printsec (PD image).*
Page 12 – March on Washington, Washington DC. 28th Aug 1963, from US Library of Congress's Prints & Photographs div. Reproduction Number: LC-DIG-ppmsca-37245. Source: loc.gov/pictures/resource/ppmsca.37245/ (PD image).
Page 13 – From *Life* Mag 4th Oct 1963. Source: books.google.com/books?id=uFIEAAAAMBAJ&printsec(PD image).*
Page 14 – Still image from the video Life In 60s Britain by Chaz Mork. Source: youtube.com/watch?v= pH0kvxCfvG8. Videographer unknown. This is a low-resolution image for information only, reproduced under fair use terms. It is believed that this image will not devalue the ability of the copyright holder to profit from the original work.
Page 15 – The Beatles on the Ed Sullivan Show, 9th Feb 1964, by CBS. Source: commons.wikimedia.org/wiki/File: Beatles_with_Ed_Sullivan. jpg. Pre-1978, no copyright mark (PD image). – Quant and Green, 1963, by Mirrorpix/Robert Young. This image is reproduced under fair use terms. It is a low-resolution image for information only. It is believed that the image will not devalue the ability of the copyright holder to profit from the original work.
Page 16 – From *Life* Mag 21st Jun 1963. Source: books.google.com/books?id=xEsEAAAAMBAJ&printsec (PD image).*
Page 17 – Lady on a London Bus, 1960. Photographer unknown. Pre-1978, no copyright mark (PD image).
– Piccadilly Circus, circa 1963. Creator unknown. Pre-1978, no copyright mark (PD image).
Page 18 – From *Life* Mag 6th Dec 1963. Source: books.google.com/books?id=T1IEAAAAMBAJ&printsec (PD image).*
Page 19 – Detail of Chevrolet advertisement, from *Life* Magazine, 14th Jun 1963. Source: books.google.com/books?id= 30sEAAAAMBAJ&printsec (PD image).* – Steaknshake, source: web.archive.org/web/20080801225201/http:/ www.steaknshake.com/history.asp. Pre-1978, no copyright mark (PD image).
Page 20 – From *Life* Mag, 15th Mar 1963. Source: books.google.com/books?id=F08EAAAAMBAJ&printsec (PD image).*
Page 21 – 1963 Mercury Monterey print ad, source: books.google.com/books?id=3kcEAAAAMBAJ&printsec. – 1963 Ford Convertible print ad, source: books.google.com/books?id=MIIEAAAAMBAJ&printsec – 1963 Dodge Dart print advertisement, source: books.google.com/books? id=IUEEAAAAMBAJ&printsec. (PD images).*
Page 22 – 1962 Fiat 1100 Series Ad from *Time* 9th Feb 1962. Source: flickr.com/photos/91591049@N00/23449288900/ by SenseiAlan. Attribution 4.0 Int (CC BY 4.0). – 1963 Renault R8, source: flickr.com/photos/ autohistorian/ 5016799 1941in/photostream. Attribution 4.0 Int (CC BY 4.0). – Volkswagen (1963) Source: pinterest.com. (PD image).*
Page 23 – From *Life* Mag, 17th May 1963. Source: books.google.com/books?id=2kgEAAAAMBAJ&printsec (PD image).*
Page 24 – From *Life* Mag 8th Nov 1963. Source: books.google.com/books?id=RVIEAAAAMBAJ&printsec (PD image).*
Page 25 – From *Life* Mag Motorola ad, 6th Oct 1961. Source: books.google.com/books?id=01MEAAAAMBAJ&printsec. (PD image).*
Page 26 – *The Lucy Show* screen still by Desilu / CBS, 6th Jan 1963.** Source: commons.wikimedia.org/ wiki/Category: The_Lucy_Show. – Van Dyke and Moore 1961, publicity image by CBS, source: en.wikipedia. org/wiki/The_Dick_Van_ Dyke_Show. Pre-1978, no copyright mark (PD image).
Page 27 – *General Hospital* publicity photo by ABC, 1963. – *Petticoat Junction* publicity photo by CBS, 1963. – Screen still from *My Favourite Martian* by CBS. – Screen still from *Doctor Who* by BBC. All images this page Pre-1978, no copyright mark. These are low-resolution image for information only, reproduced under fair use terms. It is believed that the images will not devalue the ability of the copyright holder to profit from the original work.
Page 28 – From *Life* Mag 1st Nov 1963. Source: books.google.com/books?id=VIIEAAAAMBAJ&printsec (PD image).*
Page 29 – Atlantic Provinces print advertisement. Source: eBay
Page 30 & 31 – Photos of President Kennedy, the motorcade and his family by Cecil W. Stoughton from the John F. Kennedy Library, Walt Cisco from Dallas Morning News, and Abbie Rowe from White House Photographs. Photo of Ruby and Oswald by Jack Beers Jr. from Dallas Morning News photographer. Source:commons.wikimedia.org/wiki/ Category:Assassination_of_John_F._Kennedy. All photos are in the Public domain.
Page 32 – From *Life* Mag, 17th May 1963. Source: books.google.com/books?id=2kgEAAAAMBAJ&printsec (PD image).*
Page 33 – Operation Dominic Swordfish, 11th May 1962, and President Kennedy signing Nuclear Test Ban Treaty 7th Oct 1963. Both photos by the Federal government of the USA, from the National Nuclear Security Administration Nevada Site Office Photo Library and The John F. Kennedy Presidential Library and Museum, Boston (PD images).
Page 34 – Gagarin, source: tass.com/society/899827 by Valentin Cheredintsev. Pre-1978, no copyright mark (PD image). – Glenn, Image Credit: NASA. Source: nasa.gov/content/astronaut-john-glenn-at-cape-Canaveral (PD image). – Tereshkova source: cultura.biografie online.it/la-prima-donna-nello-spazio/.
Page 35 – Green Beret in Vietnam, 1961, from Life Magazine. Source: sofrep.com/news/jfk-sends-400-green-beret-special-advisors-may-1961-begin-vietnam-involvement/. Pre-1978 (PD image). – US choppers, 1962, from Life Magazine. Source: 1960sdaysofrage.wordpress.com/2017/10/24/operation-chopper/. Pre-1978 (PD image).
Page 36 – From *Life* Mag, 20th Dec 1963. Source: books.google.com./books?id=ZIIEAAAAMBAJ&printsec (PD image).*
Page 37 – From *Life* Mag, 17th May 1963. Source: books.google.com/books?id=2kgEAAAAMBAJ&printsec (PD image).*
Page 38 – The Children's Crusade & Detroit Walk for Freedom, creators unknown. Pre-1978, no mark (PD image).

Page 39 – Wallace at the University of Alabama & Hood and Malone by AP. These images are reproduced under fair use terms. They are Pre-1978, no copyright mark. These are low-resolution image for information only and are relevant to the article. It is believed that the images will not devalue the ability of the copyright holder to profit from the original work. – Kennedy at the Oval Office. This image is the work of an employee of the United States Government (PD image).

Page 40 –March on Washington by photographer Leffler, Warren K., LC-DIG-ppmsca-04296 from the Library of Congress, and unknown photographer image from the National Archives and Records Administration. (NAID) 542055. – Martin Luther King delivering speech, creator unknown. – Kennedy and leaders of the March from the National Archives and Records Administration, (NAID) 194276. All images this page are Public Domain images.

Page 41 – From *Life* Mag, 8th Nov 1963. Source: books.google.com/books?id=RVIEAAAAMBAJ&printsec (PD image).*

Page 42 – Mandela, source: commons.wikimedia.org/wiki/Category:Nelson_Mandela. Attribution (CC BY-SA 2.0).

Page 43 – From *Life* Mag 7th Dec 1963. Source: books.google.com/books?id=H1IEAAAAMBAJ&printsec (PD image).*

Page 44 – Profumo, Keeler & Ivanov, photo creators unknown. Pre-1978, no copyright marks. Where images are not in the public domain they are reproduced here under USA Fair Use laws due to: 1- images are low resolution copies; 2- images do not devalue the ability of the copyright holders to profit from the original works in any way; 3- Images are too small to be used to make illegal copies for use in another book; 4- The images are relevant to the article.

Page 45 – Screen still from *The Great Train Robbery* by BBC, 1963**. – Ronnie Biggs Buckingham Constabulary mug shot, 1964. Source: en.wikipedia.org/wiki/File:Ronnie_Biggs_ Buckingham_Constabulary_mugshot_1960s.jpg. This image is the work of the UK government (PD image).

Page 46 – Honda print advertisement. Source: eBay

Page 47 – Movie poster for Ocean's 11, by Warner Bros, 1960.** – Sinatra publicity photo by CBS. 1966, and Martin, Garland, Sinatra from The Judy Garland Show in 1962.** Source: commons.wikimedia.org/wiki/Category:Frank_Sinatra.

Page 48 – Screen still from *Bye Bye Birdie* by Columbia Pictures, 1963**. – Jackie Chan, creator and date unknown. Pre-1978, no copyright mark (PD image).

Page 49 – Movie poster for *Irma la Dolce* by United Artists/Mirisch, 1963**. – Movie poster for *It's a Mad, Mad, Mad, Mad World* by United Artists, 1963**. – Movie poster for *Charade* by Universal Pictures, 1963**.

Page 50 & 51 – Screen stills from *Cleopatra*, 20th Century Fox, 1963**.

Page 52 – From *Life* Mag 10th May 1963. Source: books.google.com/books?id=P0kEAAAAMBAJ&source (PD image).*

Page 53 – The Beatles in Milan, 1965. Source: it.wikipedia.org/wiki/File:Beatles_duomo. Photographer unknown. Pre-1978, no copyright mark (PD image). – Patsy Cline publicity photo for Decca Records, 1960. ** Source- commons.wikimedia.org/ wiki/Category:Patsy_Cline. – The Rolling Stones at Schiphol, Amsterdam, 8th Aug 1964 by Gelderen, Hugo van/Anefo. Source: commons.wikimedia.org/wiki/Category:The_Rolling_Stones_in_1964. Pre-1978. no mark (PD image).

Page 54 – The Beach Boys, billboard advertisement. Source: commons.wikimedia.org/wiki/Category:The_Beach_Boys. – Paul and Paula, unknown creator, circa 1963. – Andy Williams, NBC TV press release, 1963. Source: commons. wikimedia.org/wiki/File:Andy_Williams_1963.JPG. All images this page are Pre-1978 no copyright mark (PD image).

Page 55 – Peter, Paul and Mary, 1963. Source: commons.wikimedia.org/wiki/Category:Peter,_Paul_and_Mary. – Leslie Gore, publicity photo. Source: commons.wikimedia.org/wiki/File:Lesley_Gore.jpg. Pre-1978 no copyright mark (PD image).

Page 56 – *National Bellas Hess* Home Shopping Catalog, Summer 1963. (PD image).*

Page 57 –2-piece suit from the Wool Bureau advertisement, from *Life* Magazine, 8th Feb 1960. Source: books.google.com/books? id=-EoEAAAAMBAJ&printsec. (PD image).* – Tea dresses from *La Pastorale* catalogue, Summer 1962. Source: likesoldclothes.tumblr.com/search/1962/. Pre-1978, no copyright mark (PD image).

Page 58 – Jacqueline Kennedy in the Diplomatic Reception Room, 5th Dec 1961 White House. Source: commons. wikimedia.org/wiki/Category:Jacqueline_Kennedy_Onassis_in_1961. Property of the US Government in the public domain. – Kennedy at the Elysee Palace, France, 31st May 1961, from the JFK Library. Source: commons.wikimedia.org/wiki/File:President_De_Gaulle_stands_between_President_ Kennedy_and_Mrs._Kennedy_on_the_steps_of_the_Elysee_Palace.jpg (PD image). – Jaqueline Kennedy at the US Embassy, New Delhi, March 12-21, 1962. Source: flickr.com/photos/54323860@N06/6914524677. Attribution-NoDerivatives 4.0 International (CC BY-ND 4.0). – Italian fashions 1960, creator unknown. Source: moda.com/fashion-history/60s-italian-fashion-1.shtml, reproduced under terms of Fair Use. Images here are significant to the article and are rendered in low resolution to avoid piracy. It is believed that these images will not in any way limit the ability of the copyright owners to sell their product.

Page 59 – From Life Mag 1st Nov 1963. Source: books.google.com/books?id=VIIEAAAAMBAJ&printsec (PD image).*

Page 60 – From Life Mag 1st Nov 1963. Source: books.google.com/books?id=VIIEAAAAMBAJ&printsec (PD image).*

Page 61 – Photo Mods of the early 1960s. Source unknown. Pre-1978 (PD image). – Models in Mary Quant mini dresses, creator unknown. Source: thedabbler.co.uk/2012/10/granny-takes-a-trip-back-in-time/. Pre-1978 (PD image). – Mary Quant, 16 December 1966. Source: commons.wikimedia.org/wiki/File:Mary_Quant_in_a_minidress_ (1966).jpg by Jac. de Nijs / Anefo. Image from the Nationaal Archief, the Dutch National Archives, licensed under the Creative Commons Attribution-Share Alike 3.0 Netherlands.

Page 62 – Penelope Tree, photographer Richard Avedon for Vogue Oct 1967. – Jean Shrimpton for Australian Vogue August 1965, Twiggy for Italian Vogue, July 1967, and various photo of Twiggy, dates, photographers, source unknown. Images reproduced this page under terms of Fair Use are used sparingly for information only, are significant to the article created and are rendered in low resolution to avoid piracy. It is believed that these images will not in any way limit the ability of the copyright owners to sell their product.

Page 63 – Models wearing fashions from the late '60s. Photographers unknown. Pre-1978, (PD images). – The Beatles. Source: commons.wikimedia.org/wiki/File:The_Beatles_magical_mystery_tour.jpg. Attribution 3.0 (CC BY 3.0).
Page 64 – From *Life* Mag 17th May 1963. Source: books.google.com/books?id=2kgEAAAAMBAJ&printsec (PD image).*
Page 65 – 727 image by Boeing, creator unknown. – Bell Touch Tone phone. Source: time.graphics/event/2311047. (PD image). – Smiley face, by Harvey Ross Ball.
Page 66 – From Life Mag 12th Jul 1963. Source: books.google.com/books?id=K1IEAAAAMBAJ&printsec (PD image).*
Page 67 – Roy Emerson by Gelderen, Hugo van / Anefo for Nationaal Archief, CC0. Number access: 2.24.01.05. Component: 915-3864. CC0 1.0 Universal (CC0 1.0) Public Domain Dedication. – Willie Mays by William C. Greene. Source: commons.wikimedia.org/wiki/Category:Willie_Mays (PD image). – Jack Nicklaus, creator unknown. Source: commons.wikimedia.org/wiki/Category:Jack_ Nicklaus. Attribution-ShareAlike 4.0 International (CC BY-SA 4.0).
Page 68 – Charles de Gaulle and Konrad Adenauer in 1958 by Ludwig Wegmann. Source: commons.wikimedia.org/wiki/ File:Charles_de_Gaulle_and_Konrad_Adenauer_%281958%29.jpg. Attribution: Bundesarchiv, B 145 Bild-F015892-0010 / Ludwig Wegmann / CC-BY-SA 3.0. – Royal Tour 1963, creator unknown. Pre-1978 no copyright mark (PD image). – Tito, unknown creator, from the Digital Library of Slovenia, reference: MJVNDGTF. Source: commons.wikimedia.org/ wiki/Josip_Broz_Tito. (PD image).
Page 69 – Pope John XXIII by Felici. Source: commons.wikimedia.org/wiki/File:Pope_John_XXIII,_1958–1963.jpg. (PD image). – Tab Cola magazine advert, creator unknown. (PD image).*
Page 70 – From *Life* Mag 13th Dec 1963. Source: books.google.com/books?id=SIIEAAAAMBAJ&printsec (PD image).*
Page 71 – From *Life* Mag 9th Aug 1963. Source: books.google.com/books?id=IIIEAAAAMBAJ&printsec (PD image).*
Page 72-74 – All photos are, where possible, CC BY 2.0 or PD images made available by the creator for free use including commercial use. Where commercial use photos are unavailable, photos are included here for information only under U.S. fair use laws due to: 1- images are low resolution copies; 2- images do not devalue the ability of the copyright holders to profit from the original works in any way; 3- Images are too small to be used to make illegal copies for use in another book; 4- The images are relevant to the article created.
Page 75 – From *Life* Mag 8th Mar 1963. Source: books.google.com/books?id=oU8EAAAAMBAJ&printsec (PD image).*
Page 78 – Western Electric print advertisement. Source: eBay.
Page 79 – Volkswagen print advertisement. Source: eBay.

*Advertisement (or image from an advertisement) is in the public domain because it was published in a collective work (such as a periodical issue) in the US between 1925 and 1977 and without a copyright notice specific to the advertisement.
**Posters for movies or events are either in the public domain (published in the US between 1925 and 1977 and without a copyright notice specific to the artwork) or owned by the production company, creator, or distributor of the movie or event. Posters, where not in the public domain, and screen stills from movies or TV shows, are reproduced here under USA Fair Use laws due to: 1- images are low resolution copies; 2- images do not devalue the ability of the copyright holders to profit from the original works in any way; 3- Images are too small to be used to make illegal copies for use in another book; 4- The images are relevant to the article created.

This book was written by Bernard Bradforsand-Tyler as part of *A Time Traveler's Guide* series of books.

All rights reserved. The author exerts the moral right to be identified as the author of the work.

No parts of this book may be reproduced, stored in any retrieval system, or transmitted in any form or by any means, without prior written permission from the author.

This is a work of nonfiction. No names have been changed, no events have been fabricated. The content of this book is provided as a source of information for the reader, however it is not meant as a substitute for direct expert opinion. Although the author has made every effort to ensure that the information in this book is correct at time of printing, and while this publication is designed to provide accurate information in regard to the subject matters covered, the author assumes no responsibility for errors, inaccuracies, omissions, or any other inconsistencies herein and hereby disclaims any liability to any party for any loss, damage, or disruption caused by errors or omissions.

All images contained herein are reproduced with the following permissions:
- Images included in the public domain.
- Images obtained under creative commons license.
- Images included under fair use terms.
- Images reproduced with owner's permission.

All image attributions and source credits are provided at the back of the book. All images are the property of their respective owners and are protected under international copyright laws.

First printed in 2022 in the USA (ISBN 978-1-922676-07-8).
Revised in 2024, 2nd Edition (ISBN 978-1-922676-40-5).
Self-published by B. Bradforsand-Tyler.

www.ingramcontent.com/pod-product-compliance
Lightning Source LLC
Chambersburg PA
CBHW072104110526
44590CB00018B/3313